Understanding
My Chameleon

Reptiles are becoming very popular pets and are overtaking cats and dogs as household members, however, their husbandry requirements are much more complex to keep them happy and healthy.

As a company who sees every day the shortfalls in caring for these specialised animals, we are pleased to endorse the series of "Reptiles are Cool" written by Siuna Reid, an experienced exotic veterinarian who cares enough to try and make a difference.

These books are very basic and provide simple steps and explanations of how and why we need to provide specialised environments for our pet reptiles to improve their captive quality of life as best we can.

—Pinmoore Animal Laboratory Services

REPTILES ARE COOL

Understanding
My Chameleon

Siuna A Reid
BVMS Cert AVP (ZM) MRCVS

Edited by
Vivienne E Lodge

Ellen, Robyn and Jenna

Forever in my heart

CONTENTS

Siuna A Reid

INTRODUCTION

I have been a vet for a long time and I have seen many changes in the kinds of animals that I treat. Over the past ten years there has been a huge increase in the number of reptiles that are kept as pets.

Reptiles are very different from mammals. The purpose of this book is to try to explain these differences and why they are important to the health and wellbeing of pet reptiles.

There are hundreds of different species of chameleons being kept as pets. The onus is on the supervising adult to research the specific requirements before buying their pet. This book explains the importance of husbandry and some of the diseases that can occur if basic needs are not fulfilled.

Reptiles carry many different bacteria, one of which is salmonella. Although not harmful to them, the bacteria can cause illness in humans. Therefore, it is essential to wash your hands thoroughly after handling all reptiles.

Later in the book you will come across the following symbols. Each one highlights a particular aspect of your reptile's care, relating directly to the health issue being discussed.

House

Furniture

Heat and Light

UV light

Water/Humidity

Food

CHAMELEONS AS PETS

Buying a pet and looking after it is a huge responsibility. As a pet owner you have to make sure that your pet has somewhere suitable to live, has the correct food to eat and receives lots of care and attention. You have to notice when your pet is not feeling well and may need to be taken to the vet.

The most commonly kept pets are mammals such as dogs, cats, rabbits and hamsters. Humans are mammals too, so we generally find it quite easy to relate to other mammals and to realise when they are unwell or in distress. If you stand on your dog's paw he will yelp and you will know he is in pain. If your dog is too cold you will notice that he is shivering and if he is too hot you will notice that he is panting. If he doesn't eat his dinner you will realise that he is feeling unwell.

You have chosen to keep a chameleon as a pet. Chameleons are reptiles and reptiles are very different from mammals. Your chameleon will not give you such obvious signals to let you know that he is feeling unwell, or too hot, or too cold, or in pain. His signs of distress are much more subtle and you will have to observe him very closely to ensure that he remains healthy. Otherwise his suffering will go unnoticed. You should weigh your chameleon regularly. It may not be obvious just from looking at him that he is losing weight.

Many of the health problems which occur in chameleons are related to some aspect of their environment or their diet. In this book we will first look at the correct housing and feeding for your chameleon. Then we will go through the body systems of your chameleon to find out how they work and what to look for should things go wrong.

3

CAPTIVE BRED

Wherever possible buy a captive bred chameleon. Chameleons bought from wild stock are often exposed to, and can carry a wide range of different parasites, bacteria and viruses. Buying a wild caught chameleon also encourages this unethical trade.

HOLIDAY CARE

Everybody needs a holiday! When choosing a suitable place for your chameleon to stay whilst you are away, ensure that he is not exposed to other chameleons. If your chameleon is either living in isolation, or in an isolated group, suddenly placing him in an environment where there are other chameleons is dangerous. There is a huge risk of disease spread. Wherever possible, arrange for your chameleon to be cared for at your own home.

INSURANCE

Please remember that chameleon health care is specialised and if they become ill treatment can be expensive. Insurance is one way to protect your chameleon.

VISITING THE VET

 At some point you may need to take your chameleon to the vet. This symbol, which you will come across throughout the book, indicates when you will need to seek extra help, medicine or maybe even surgery for your chameleon. Try to choose a vet who has a special interest in reptiles. Some vets take more exams so that they have extra qualifications for treating reptiles. If your local vets are not reptile enthusiasts they should be able to recommend a vet who is. If you have difficulty finding a suitable vet you could contact The Royal College of Veterinary Surgeons www.rcvs.org.uk.

THE HOUSE

Where will your chameleon live? You will need to buy a specialised mesh vivarium for him to use as his house. It is best to get this (and also the things that you put inside it – see below) from a specialist reptile shop. Chameleons need a much lower humidity level than other reptiles. Mesh houses allow the air to flow through. The house also needs to be tall as most chameleons live in trees and like to climb. Dwarf chameleons are an exception as they live on the forest floor.

Within the house you are trying to create a world which mimics the environment your type of chameleon would live in in the wild. Meller's chameleon is a large chameleon and needs a lot of space, whereas dwarf species like Brookesia live on the forest floor. Therefore it is very important that you fully research your chosen species so that you can create the correct living environment.

It is also important to think about where within your home you will place the chameleon's house. The best place is in a room that is used, like your bedroom or the main living room. Your chameleon needs to be somewhere with a constant temperature. Do not put his house beside a window or over a radiator as the temperature will rise and fall too much in these areas.

SUBSTRATE & FURNITURE

Substrate is the material used to cover the floor of your chameleon's house. Bark chippings, or a combination of soil and moss make a good floor covering. You will also need to put some furniture in his house. He needs to have somewhere to hide, especially if his house is in a busy room. Plants such as vines can also be used as hiding areas. Natural plants look good in a house, but it is also possible to use plastic plants which have the added advantage of being washable.

HEAT AND LIGHT

Life on Earth is supported by the sun. The sun provides heat and also light. Animals' need both heat and light to survive.

Mammals can control their own body temperature. The food they eat provides the body with energy and heat. If they are too cold they shiver and if they are too hot they sweat. These processes use a lot of energy.

Your chameleon is a reptile and reptiles regulate their body temperature very differently from mammals. This is a major and vitally important difference. Reptiles are cold blooded (exothermic). This means that their bodies cannot produce heat from the food that they eat. Because of this they need much less energy from food to survive. A 100g reptile needs only 5% of the energy that a 100g mammal needs. To keep warm they need to bathe in the sun or sit on a warm rock. They have no hair, no sweat glands and do not shiver. This means that your chameleon will show no obvious signs that they are too hot or too cold.

You need to provide sources of heat for your chameleon within his house. This could be a heat bulb, or a ceramic bulb. It is important that you know the temperature in both the hottest and the coolest areas. To do this you will need to use thermometers around their house. A thermostat is a device that should be added to the house to control the temperature.

If you are not aware of the temperature in your chameleon's house there is a danger that he could become too hot. As he cannot sweat to cool off, or remove layers of clothing as we would, he will try to hide in a cooler part of his tank. Providing a water bath is a good idea.

However, it is more common for a chameleon to find himself in an environment which is too cold. Cooler temperatures are unlikely to kill him, but will put a strain on his body and organs. His muscles, lungs, intestines and heart will struggle to work if they are too cold, and if this goes on for a long time it can lead to illness and even death.

ULTRA VIOLET LIGHT

 As well as producing heat and light, the sun also produces ultraviolet (UV) light. This is a type of light which we cannot see but chameleons can. It affects the skin of humans and can cause sunburn.

Reptiles use UV light to make vitamin D3. This helps to keep their bones strong and healthy and enables their guts to absorb calcium from their food. To obtain vitamin D3 he will need exposure to UV light for 12 hours a day.

If your chameleon does not receive enough vitamin D3 his bones will become soft and they might even snap and break. He may develop twitchy toes caused by faulty muscle contractions.

Ultra violet light can be provided as a combination bulb or a UV tube. The tube needs to be no more than 30cm away from your chameleon. Remember that a UV tube will not provide him with any heat. The bulb should be changed once a year. This is because although the bulb may appear to be working, over time it will eventually stop making UV light.

WATER

 Chameleons are quite specialised when it comes to drinking. Most species drink the water as it drips from the leaves in the house. Spraying the plants with a plant spray three times a day, or buying an automated spraying system are both ways of making sure your chameleon has access to enough water. Without water his body will become dehydrated and this can lead to constipation. It may sound unusual, but if your chameleon were to become constipated he could die.

Humidity is also an important consideration when setting up your chameleon's house. When water evaporates it forms an invisible gas called water vapour. Humidity is a measure of the amount of water vapour that is present in the air.

In hot dry areas, like deserts, there is not a lot of water vapour in the air which means that deserts have low humidity. Rain forests are also hot but they have lots of water vapour in the air and so they have high humidity.

The level of humidity required for your chameleon will depend on his particular species and the type of environment he needs to live in. You must use a hygrometer to measure the level of humidity in your chameleon's house to ensure that it is suitable for him.

FOOD

Most chameleons eat insects. In the wild a chameleon would eat whatever insects he could catch, depending on the season. In captivity you will need to buy live insects for him to eat.

Most of the insects that are fed to pet chameleons are mass reared. Traditionally, locusts, black and brown crickets, meal worms and wax worms have been fed. Mario worms and calci worms can also be obtained. This is a very artificial situation and we are greatly simplifying our chameleons' diets by offering them only a few types of insects to eat.

All insects are very low in vitamins and minerals. When you buy your crickets or other insects from the supplier, they are often hungry and have eaten their cardboard containers. This further reduces their mineral content. You can boost the mineral levels by feeding some dry fish flakes or small amounts of greens, such as dandelions to your live food. Dusting the insects with calcium/vitamin D3 powder before feeding them to your chameleon will also help. This will ensure that he receives adequate amounts of these minerals in his diet.

Don't be afraid to catch other insects, for example moths or spiders to feed to your chameleon. These will be packed full of nutrients and will be better for him than the commercially produced live food. If you catch insects from your garden make sure that it hasn't been treated with chemicals.

The frequency with which you feed your chameleon will depend on his age and stage of development. It is important not to put too many live insects into his house at one time. Some of them might bite his skin, which will cause pain and damage. They can also be highly annoying and cause your chameleon to become agitated and unhappy. So if he is not hungry, take the live food out and try again later. There is nothing worse than having your dinner sitting on your head!

SKIN

The skin is the largest organ of the body. Reptile skin is unique and has many functions which include protecting the body, providing camouflage and making vitamin D3. Chameleons have special cells in the skin called chromatophores. These allow the chameleon to change colour. Colour changes are the result of mood changes or potential threats.

SHEDDING (ECDYSIS)

When mammals grow, their skin stretches and grows too. Reptiles are different. Their skin does not stretch with growth. Therefore the ability to shed skin is very important to your chameleon. When it is time to shed, your chameleon will produce a chemical which divides the old and the new skin. At this stage his skin will look dull and bluish. He will naturally rub himself against rough or moist furniture to remove his old skin in large pieces. You will now see his shiny and colourful new skin start to appear.

It is advisable to keep a diary of how often your chameleon sheds.

Sometimes chameleons have problems shedding. This is known as dysecdysis. It is one of the most common reasons for visiting the vet.

Make sure that the temperature in your chameleon's house is correct. If it is too cold he will struggle to shed.

Lack of humidity is one of the most common reasons for failure to shed. You can increase the humidity by spraying the tank with water. Just make sure it does not become too wet as this can lead to ulcers forming on the skin.

Any problems relating to shedding should be closely monitored and may require a visit to the vet.

SKIN PROBLEMS

ABSCESSES

Abscesses are lumps on the skin which are infected with bacteria or fungi. Damaged skin is a common cause of infection.

15

Check for sharp objects in the house.

Correct temperature will help your chameleon fight off infection

A good diet keeps the immune system healthy.

Make sure all furniture has smooth edges.

If your chameleon does develops an abscess he will need to have an operation to remove it. Fungal infections are very difficult to treat. A considerable amount of medicine may be needed to cure any disease.

Thermal burns happen when chameleons come into contact with an unprotected hot surface. This could be a heat lamp or a hot rock. Chameleons seem to have difficulty detecting hot surfaces and do not react until serious damage has already been done to their skin.

Always check that any bulbs, heat pads or hot rocks in your chameleon's house are working correctly to prevent burning. If the heat bulb is inside the house always ensure that it has a wire cage around it.

Minor burns may not need any treatment. However, serious burns will need veterinary care. This treatment may include creams and antibiotics.

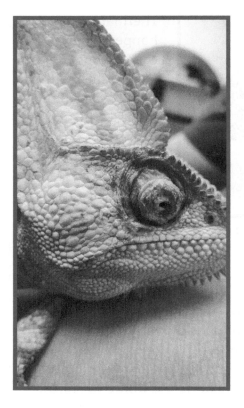

Poor diet can affect the skin. Vitamin A is very important to chameleons skin. Too little of it makes the skin of the eyes and mouth become swollen. Poor sight will make it very difficult to see and therefore feeding becomes a challenge. Too much vitamin A in the diet causes the skin to become thickened and flaky.

A diet with low calcium and low vitamin D3, but with lots of fat, can result in the body growing too quickly. This leads to weak bones and skin that sheds over and over again.

To help your chameleon make vitamin D3 his UV bulb needs to have the correct strength and be placed in the correct position.

Make sure you feed a balanced diet to your chameleon to ensure he receives an adequate amount of nutrients, vitamins and minerals to keep his skin healthy. Remember to feed his live food on greens and fish food flakes. Also dust the live food with a calcium supplement before feeding to your chameleon.

18

Most nutritional diseases require veterinary assistance.

MITES

Look for little black or red dots on the skin. The mites breed in the house. They bite the skin which becomes very itchy. Affected chameleons are often restless and will rub their face and skin.

The house will need to be cleaned thoroughly to get rid of all the mites and their eggs. Don't take your chameleon to a pet shop when you go on holiday. Mites can spread very easily.

The furniture will need to be cleaned and fresh substrate placed in the house.

The vet will be able to give you flea medicine to kill the mites.

Gangrene is seen commonly in chameleons. There are two types of gangrene, wet and dry. Dry gangrene is the most common and is caused by bacteria that invade the skin causing it to die. It is seen in the tail, the hands and the feet. Untreated gangrene may cause your chameleon to lose a toe or even a whole foot.

Make sure there are no sharp edges in the house or on the furniture which may cut the chameleon. Keep an eye on any house mates to make sure they are not fighting.

The correct temperature helps the chameleon to fight infection.

Gangrene needs surgical and medical treatment by the vet.

20

EYES

Chameleons have extremely good eyes that see colour and also ultra violet light.

Chameleon eyelids are quite different to ours. If you look at your own eye you will see that you have a big upper eyelid which comes down to cover your eye when you blink, and a much smaller lower eyelid. In chameleons the upper eyelid is smaller and the lower eyelid is bigger and stronger. Chameleons also have a third eyelid which sweeps across the surface of the eye to clean it when they blink.

Chameleons are unusual as they can move each eye independently. This allows them to catch prey more easily and also spot predators.

The coloured circle in your eye is called the iris. This deterimines whether you have green, blue or brown eyes. The pupil is in the centre of the iris. Your pupil is black and round. It can become bigger or smaller depending the amount of light around you.

Chameleons have round pupils as they are a species that is awake during the day. Unlike us, your chameleon can move his iris if he wants to.

Chameleons have tiny bones in the white part of their eyes called scleral ossicles. These help to give the eyeball extra strength.

EYE PROBLEMS

CONJUNCTIVITIS

Conjunctivitis is an inflammation of the eyelids. It is often caused by a bacterial infection.

Low temperatures in your chameleon's house will reduce the ability to fight infection.

 A balanced diet will help fight infection.

 Conjunctivitis should be treated with antibiotics.

HYPOVITAMINOSIS A

A diet lacking in vitamin A can lead to swelling of the eyelids.

 Feed a balanced diet with sufficient vitamin A to prevent eye problems.

TRAUMA (DAMAGE)

 Any trauma to your chameleon's eye could result in serious damage. This could happen in several ways. Examples would be, bedding caught in the eye or a scratch caused by a sharp object. An ulcer may form on the cornea. This is the transparent outer layer of the eye. Ulcers are very painful and in severe cases may cause the eye to burst.

To prevent eye trauma you should check your chameleon's house and furniture carefully for any sharp objects. Remember to take extra care when handling your chameleon outside of his house. Cage mates can also inflict serious damage if they fight.

Take care when selecting a UV light for your chameleon's house. Inferior lights can emit harmful rays which could burn his eyes.

If you suspect your chameleon has suffered any trauma to his eye take him to the vet immediately. Eye damage is an emergency and if not treated in time, your chameleon may lose his eye.

DIGESTIVE SYSTEM

The digestive system is the part of the body that converts food into energy. Left over waste is expelled through the vent.

The digestive tract of your chameleon consists of the mouth, stomach, intestines and vent. The vent is the reptile equivalent of the anus in mammals.

MOUTH

 Chameleons have lots of very small bones that are similar to teeth. If they break a tooth it will not regrow. Other lizards can regrow broken teeth. In our mouths the roof is called the hard palate. The chameleon does not have a roof to his mouth. Instead he has a hole called the choana. Their tongue is unique and shoots from the mouth to catch insects. The end of the tongue is a bit like a sucker.

STOMACH

A tube called the oesophagus leads from the mouth to the stomach.

INTESTINES

After the stomach the digestive tract continues as the small and large intestine.

VENT

The vent is made up of three areas. The food waste from the large intestine is stored in the coprodeum. The urodeum is the area which stores urine, and sperm or eggs (depending on whether your chameleon is male or female). Both the coprodeum and urodeum empty into the proctodeum and from here all faeces and urine are passed out of the vent.

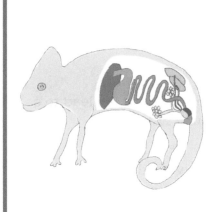

- liver
- stomach
- small and large intestine
- pancreas
- urodeum (area where urine is stored and where eggs and sperm are collected)
- copradeum (area where faeces is stored)
- proctodeum (area where all waste is stored before leaving the vent)

LIVER

The liver is the largest organ inside the body and has many functions. It plays an important part in the breakdown of proteins and fats from the food. It helps the body to expel any poisons and other harmful substances.

PANCREAS

The pancreas produces juices which help to breakdown food.

PROBLEMS OF THE DIGESTIVE SYSTEM

STOMATITIS

Stomatitis is an inflammation of the mouth. It is commonly known as mouth rot. Stomatitis can be caused by viral or bacterial infection. It can also be caused by damage to the mouth. This is not common in chameleons.

Pay particular attention to the condition of the house.

Low temperatures in the house can lead to a weakening the immune system.

Check the furniture in your chameleon's house to make sure that there are no sharp areas which could damage his mouth.

If you think your chameleon might have stomatitis have him checked by the vet.

FATTY LIVER DISEASE

Chameleons need to eat regularly. Fatty liver disease is also known as hepatic lipidosis. Liver cells become swamped with fat, preventing the liver from working properly. It is very difficult to detect fatty liver disease. There are no obvious symptoms but a chameleon with this condition will stop eating. It is important to weigh your chameleon regularly to spot any severe weight loss.

Low temperature can cause loss of appetite.

If the food for your chameleon is too big, or if you feed too many insects at once, this can put him off eating. Make sure you are feeding a good balanced diet for your particular species of chameleon.

If your chameleon loses more than 10% of his bodyweight you should take him to the vet.

IMPACTION AND CONSTIPATION

Chameleons often eat material from the floor of their house by mistake. This can lead to impaction in the large intestine. This is when pieces of material clump together and cause a blockage. Constipation is when the chameleon cannot pass faeces. You may notice him straining to pass faeces or that his faeces look very dry.

The temperature in your chameleon's house is vital. If it is too cold the intestines cannot digest food properly and this can lead to constipation.

29

Calcium is needed to make the intestines work properly. Ensure that your chameleon's UV light is at the correct height and is not too old.

It is very important that your chameleon has water at all times and that the humidity in his house is at the correct level. Dehydration often leads to constipation.

Be sure your chameleon is eating the correct type and amount of food. If he is greedy his intestines may become too full and therefore prone to impaction.

Ensure the material you use for the floor of the house is large enough not to be swallowed by a hungry chameleon.

This condition is often left until it is too late. If an impaction is very severe an operation may be necessary to remove the material blocking the intestine.

A prolapse happens when one of the organs plumbed into the vent, (for example the large intestine) gets pushed out of the body. Egg binding and a low calcium diet can cause a vent prolapse.

This is an emergency. If you suspect a prolapse you must take your chameleon to the vet as soon as possible.

LUNGS

Inside the bodies of mammals there is a big sheet of muscle, called the diaphragm. This separates the chest, where the lungs are, and the abdomen, where the stomach and intestines are. Your chameleon has no diaphragm. His chest and abdomen share the same space.

Partly because they have no diaphragm chameleons are unable to cough. This can be a problem because if they get a build-up of fluid in their lungs, they are unable to clear it by coughing.

LUNG PROBLEMS

PNEUMONIA

Pneumonia is an inflammation and infection of the lungs. It is not common in chameleons but can develop as a result of poor housing.

  It is vital that the reptile house is kept at the correct temperature and has the correct level of humidity.

A good diet protects the immune system.

 If your chameleon is showing signs of illness then you must take him to the vet.

33

HEART

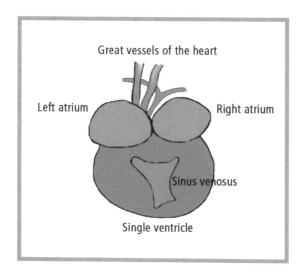

Great vessels of the heart

Left atrium

Right atrium

Sinus venosus

Single ventricle

The heart is a specialised muscle which collects blood full of oxygen from the lungs and pumps it around the body. It also collects blood full of carbon dioxide from the body and pumps it back to the lungs. This cycle goes on continuously.

The heart sits in the chest cavity in mammals and is divided into four chambers. The right atrium collects blood full of carbon dioxide from the body, sends it down to the right ventricle which then pumps it to the lungs. The left atrium collects blood full of oxygen from the lungs, sends it down to the left ventricle which pumps it around the body. Blood is constantly being pumped from right to left, via the lungs and travels around the body inside a series of tubes of varying diameters. These are known as blood vessels.

The heart of a chameleon differs from the heart of a mammal in several ways. It is especially adapted to suit the life of a reptile. In chameleons, the heart sits forward in the chest, between the front legs. Inside the heart of the chameleon there are three chambers. These are the right atrium, left

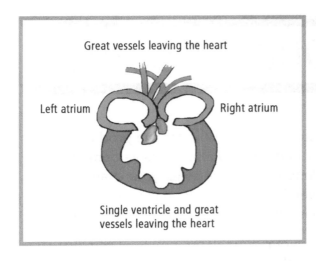

Great vessels leaving the heart

Left atrium

Right atrium

Single ventricle and great
vessels leaving the heart

atrium and the ventricle. There is also an extra chamber outside the heart, called the sinus venosus which collects blood. Chameleons can move blood to wherever it is needed in the body. Remember how our mammal hearts always pump blood round the body from right to left? Chameleons can change the direction of the blood so that it can flow backwards. This is one of the ways that chameleons can survive if they are short of oxygen or if they become dehydrated.

When a house is too cold, the heart cannot beat fast enough to keep the blood pumping to all the vital organs.

It is vital to provide a good source of UV light and a balanced diet.

The heart is a muscle and needs a constant supply of calcium to enable it to beat properly.

Heart disease is not commonly diagnosed in chameleons.

REPRODUCTIVE SYSTEM

The reproductive system is responsible for the production of sperm or eggs, for mating, and also the development of offspring. It varies depending on whether your chameleon is male or female. Even if your chameleon lives alone the reproductive system is still active and can develop problems.

Determining whether your chameleon is male or female will depend on the species that you have. Some chameleons, like the Yemen have extra toes on the back feet. This will be a male. Another difference is larger head horns on the male. With other chameleon species it is much more difficult to tell the difference between male and female.

MALES

Male chameleons have two testicles which produce sperm. They are inside the body and near the kidneys. Instead of having one penis (willy) like mammals, they have two. These are called hemipenes and are found inside the vent. Only one hemipene is used at a time for mating. The hemipenes do not carry urine the way that a mammals penis does.

HEMIPENE PROBLEMS

PROLAPSE

The hemipenes are normally inside the vent and only come out for mating. If a hemipene gets stuck outside the body this is known as a prolapse. A prolapsed hemipene can become damaged and infected.

 If you think your chameleon has a prolapsed hemipene he needs to go to the vet. If the hemipene has suffered a lot of damage or has become infected he may need to have an operation to remove it.

ABSCESS

Sometimes a hemipene can become impacted with hard pus, forming an abscess. This is a common condition in male chameleons.

 It is important to keep his house at the correct temperature.

A good balanced diet will promote a healthy immune system, helping to fight infection.

If you suspect your chameleon has an abscessed hemipene you will need to take him to the vet. He may need an operation to remove the abscess or the hemipene.

Note that if a chameleon does need to have a hemipene removed he will still be able to breed, as he will be able to use his other hemipene.

FEMALES

Female chameleons have two ovaries which produce eggs. They are found inside the body near the kidneys. They also have two oviducts. These are tubes along which the eggs are transported to the urodeum area of the vent. Chameleons tend to lay large numbers of rubbery eggs. If the male and female susccessfully mate the eggs will hatch in approximately 6 to 18 months, depending on the species. However, female chameleons can produce eggs without mating and sometimes this can lead to problems.

EGG PROBLEMS

FOLLICULAR STASIS AND EGG BINDING

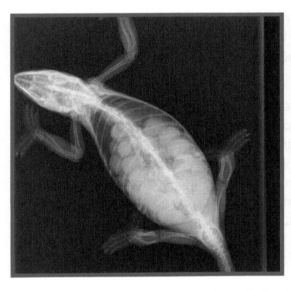

Follicular stasis is a condition where the eggs do not develop properly and are without a shell. These undeveloped eggs remain inside the body and can make an affected chameleon very ill.

Egg binding is common in female chameleons. Here the eggs have been made and are fully developed but they become stuck inside the body and cannot be laid. The picture shows an egg bound chameleon.

 The house must be kept at the correct temperature. If it is too cold her body will struggle to make and lay eggs.

 Dehydration will make it very difficult for your female chameleon to make and lay eggs.

Making eggs uses a large amount of energy. Ensure that your chameleon has an adequate and balanced diet.

Your female chameleon will need a hiding place in her house with plenty of substrate. This allows her to dig holes where she will bury her eggs.

If your female chameleon develops any egg related problems she will need to visit the vet. Egg bound chameleons need an operation to remove the retained eggs from the body. Follicular stasis can only be corrected by spaying. This is an operation to remove the ovaries and oviducts.

KIDNEYS

- kidneys & ureters
- ovaries or testicles
- urodeum (area where urine is stored and where eggs and sperm are collected)
- copradeum (area where faeces is stored)
- proctodeum (area where all waste is stored before leaving the vent)

Mammals and chameleons have two kidneys. The purpose of the kidneys is to remove poisonous waste material from the body.

THE MAMMAL KIDNEY

All fluid taken in by the body is processed by the kidneys. These include cups of tea, soft drinks and of course water. The kidney ensures that there is enough water to keep the body hydrated. Any water not required is stored in the bladder until it is passed as urine, which is a clear and yellow liquid.

THE REPTILE KIDNEY

The kidney of the reptile is different as it does not have the ability to retain water within the body. Reptile urine is a mixture of water and a solid white material called uric acid.

The chameleon has developed unique ways to keep his body hydrated.

There is a small flap inside the urodeum that can move water into the large bowel where it is reabsorbed into the body. The chameleon can also suck water up through the vent whilst bathing. Their urine is stored in the urodeum and passes out of the body through the vent.

KIDNEY PROBLEMS

GOUT

Gout is a condition caused by too much uric acid in the body. The uric acid presents itself as solid white material which can easily be spotted in the urine. Sometimes these hard crystals deposit themselves in the muscles, joints and organs which can cause damage.

 Make sure your chameleon always has enough water to drink. Dehydration can contribute to the development of gout.

 Feed a balanced nutritious diet to your chameleon to prevent gout.

Gout is serious and will need veterinary treatment.

KIDNEY FAILURE

There are many causes of kidney failure. These may include infections, inflammation and toxic damage. A chameleon with kidney failure will be less active than usual, lose his appetite, suffer weight loss and become dehydrated.

 The house must be at the correct temperature.

 Your chameleon needs to have access to drinking water.

 Correct diet is important. Do not over dust the insects with calcium powder as this can also damage the kidneys. A good diet also helps to support the immune system.

 Any weight loss or change in eating habits needs a visit to the vet.

NUTRITIONAL DISEASE

Nutritional diseases are caused by an incorrect diet. They can occur if fed too much or too little of the nutrients, vitamins and minerals needed to maintain good health. Nutritional disease is a common problem seen in chameleons, yet it is preventable.

MALNUTRITION

Malnutrition is a result of poor diet. This may be too much or too little of any food. The photograph shows a chameleon suffering from malnutrition.

Keeping your chameleon at the correct temperature helps his stomach and small intestine to absorb all the nutrients from his food.

44

Your chameleon needs a good source of UV light to help his body absorb calcium from the intestine.

 Make sure you feed a varied diet to your chameleon.

 Most cases of malnutrition need specialist veterinary care.

VITAMIN A DEFICIENCY

 Vitamin A is needed to keep the insides of the mouth, the eyes and kidneys working. Lack of this vitamin can cause thickening of the eyelids, as shown in the photograph. It can also lead to kidney failure.

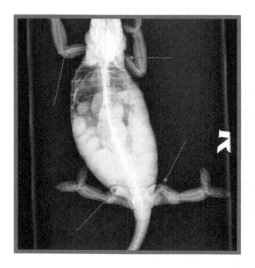

Vitamin D3 and calcium are needed to keep your chameleon's bones strong and his muscles active. An insufficiency will lead to the bones becoming soft and bendy. They may even break. The chameleon in the x ray has no calcium in the skeleton and has several breaks (fractures) in the long bones of the legs shown by the green arrows.

Keeping your chameleon at the correct temperature helps his stomach and small intestine to absorb all the nutrients from his food.

Your chameleon needs a good source of UV light to help his body absorb calcium from the intestine.

Make sure you feed a varied diet to your chameleon.

If your chameleon has a nutritional disease he may have to visit the vet for vitamin injections and extra help with feeding.

PARASITES

Parasites are creatures that feed off another animal. There are two basic types of parasites. Internal parasites live inside the body. External parasites live on the outside.

One example of an internal parasite is roundworm as seen in the photograph above. Roundworms and tapeworms are found inside the intestines. Mites and ticks are external parasites that suck the blood and bite the skin.

If you see any moving black or red dots on your chameleon's skin, or worms in his faeces, you need to take him to the vet. These are signs of parasites.

INFECTIOUS DISEASE

There are a number of viruses that can affect chameleons. Fortunately these are not common. Irido virus is carried by insects and can sometimes make chameleons unwell. Buying captive bred chameleons and choosing holiday accommodation carefully reduces the risk of infection.

Bacteria and fungus can also be infectious.

 Infections need treatment from a vet. Act quickly if you have a collection of reptiles to try to prevent spreading.

GROWTHS, TRAUMA & AUTOTOMY

GROWTHS

If you find any lump or swelling on your chameleon take him to the vet. To find out exactly what the growth is the vet may need to do some tests. It might be a tumour and some tumours are types of cancer that can spread. However, the lumps may be abscesses or cysts. Some growths can be surgically removed.

TRAUMA

If your chameleon has suffered any trauma or injury he must be taken to the vet to be checked and to receive any necessary treatment.

AUTOTOMY

Autotomy is the ability to drop or shed the tail. Chameleons do not have this defence mechanism. If the tail is damaged and needs amputating, it will not grow back.

Any serious injuries need to be checked by the vet.

NEUROLOGICAL DISEASE

The brain and the spinal chord in chameleons are similar to those found in mammals.

LOW CALCIUM (HYPOCALCAEMIA)

Low calcium in the diet can cause muscular tremors. Sometimes called 'piano playing', when the toes are seen to twitch when the rest of the body remains still.

 Ensure the house is warm to help the digestion process of food.

 It is vital to have a good quality UV bulb at the correct distance to maximise calcium absorption.

 A good balanced diet with calcium and vitamin supplements is essential to make sure the muscles work correctly.

 A low calcium condition needs regular calcium injections.

INDEX

M

mites 19
mouth 18, 25, 26, 27, 28, 45
mouth rot 27

N

neurological disease 51
nutritional disease 46

O

oesophagus 26
ovaries 41
oxygen 34, 35

P

pancreas 27
parasites 47
penis 37
pneumonia 32
proctodeum 26, 27, 41
prolapse 31, 37

R

reproductive system 36
roundworms 47

S

scleral ossicles 22
shedding (ecdysis) 15
sinus venosus 35
skin 10, 13, 14, 15, 17, 18, 19, 20, 47
sperm 27, 41
spinal chord 51
stomach 27
stomatitis 27, 28